Release It!

The Little Book For Release Info

Created & Designed By
TeeCee Design Studio

Book Title: ____

Release Date: ____

Cover Reveal: ____

ARC Release: ____

Send to Pre-Reader(s) By: ____

Send to Blogs By: ____

Send to Betas By: ____

Send to Editor By: ____

Send to Formatter By: ____

Set Up Pre-Order/Release By: ____

Final Cover Design Needed By: ____

Upload By: ____

Extra Notes:

____

____

____

____

Book Title: ___________________________________

Release Date: ___________________________________

Cover Reveal: ___________________________________

ARC Release: ___________________________________

Send to Pre-Reader(s) By: ___________________________________

Send to Blogs By: ___________________________________

Send to Betas By: ___________________________________

Send to Editor By: ___________________________________

Send to Formatter By: ___________________________________

Set Up Pre-Order/Release By: ___________________________________

Final Cover Design Needed By: ___________________________________

Upload By: ___________________________________

Extra Notes:

____

____

____

____

____

Book Title: ___________________________

Release Date: ___________________________

Cover Reveal: ___________________________

ARC Release: ___________________________

Send to Pre-Reader(s) By: ___________________________

Send to Blogs By: ___________________________

Send to Betas By: ___________________________

Send to Editor By: ___________________________

Send to Formatter By: ___________________________

Set Up Pre-Order/Release By: ___________________________

Final Cover Design Needed By: ___________________________

Upload By: ___________________________

Extra Notes:

____

____

____

____

Book Title: ____

Release Date: ____

Cover Reveal: ____

ARC Release: ____

Send to Pre-Reader(s) By: ____

Send to Blogs By: ____

Send to Betas By: ____

Send to Editor By: ____

Send to Formatter By: ____

Set Up Pre-Order/Release By: ____

Final Cover Design Needed By: ____

Upload By: ____

Extra Notes:

____

____

____

____

____

Book Title: _______________________________

Release Date: _______________________________

Cover Reveal: _______________________________

ARC Release: _______________________________

Send to Pre-Reader(s) By: _______________________________

Send to Blogs By: _______________________________

Send to Betas By: _______________________________

Send to Editor By: _______________________________

Send to Formatter By: _______________________________

Set Up Pre-Order/Release By: _______________________________

Final Cover Design Needed By: _______________________________

Upload By: _______________________________

Extra Notes:

____

____

____

____

____

Book Title: ______________________________

Release Date: ______________________________

Cover Reveal: ______________________________

ARC Release: ______________________________

Send to Pre-Reader(s) By: ______________________________

Send to Blogs By: ______________________________

Send to Betas By: ______________________________

Send to Editor By: ______________________________

Send to Formatter By: ______________________________

Set Up Pre-Order/Release By: ______________________________

Final Cover Design Needed By: ______________________________

Upload By: ______________________________

Extra Notes:

____

____

____

____

____

Book Title: ___________________________________

Release Date: ___________________________________

Cover Reveal: ___________________________________

ARC Release: ___________________________________

Send to Pre-Reader(s) By: ___________________________________

Send to Blogs By: ___________________________________

Send to Betas By: ___________________________________

Send to Editor By: ___________________________________

Send to Formatter By: ___________________________________

Set Up Pre-Order/Release By: ___________________________________

Final Cover Design Needed By: ___________________________________

Upload By: ___________________________________

Extra Notes:

____

____

____

____

____

Book Title: ___________________________________

Release Date: ___________________________________

Cover Reveal: ___________________________________

ARC Release: ___________________________________

Send to Pre-Reader(s) By: ___________________________________

Send to Blogs By: ___________________________________

Send to Betas By: ___________________________________

Send to Editor By: ___________________________________

Send to Formatter By: ___________________________________

Set Up Pre-Order/Release By: ___________________________________

Final Cover Design Needed By: ___________________________________

Upload By: ___________________________________

Extra Notes:

____

____

____

____

____

Book Title: ____

Release Date: ____

Cover Reveal: ____

ARC Release: ____

Send to Pre-Reader(s) By: ____

Send to Blogs By: ____

Send to Betas By: ____

Send to Editor By: ____

Send to Formatter By: ____

Set Up Pre-Order/Release By: ____

Final Cover Design Needed By: ____

Upload By: ____

Extra Notes:

____

____

____

____

____

Book Title: _______________________________

Release Date: _______________________________

Cover Reveal: _______________________________

ARC Release: _______________________________

Send to Pre-Reader(s) By: _______________________________

Send to Blogs By: _______________________________

Send to Betas By: _______________________________

Send to Editor By: _______________________________

Send to Formatter By: _______________________________

Set Up Pre-Order/Release By: _______________________________

Final Cover Design Needed By: _______________________________

Upload By: _______________________________

Extra Notes:

____

____

____

____

____

Book Title: ____

Release Date: ____

Cover Reveal: ____

ARC Release: ____

Send to Pre-Reader(s) By: ____

Send to Blogs By: ____

Send to Betas By: ____

Send to Editor By: ____

Send to Formatter By: ____

Set Up Pre-Order/Release By: ____

Final Cover Design Needed By: ____

Upload By: ____

Extra Notes:

____

____

____

____

Book Title: ____

Release Date: ____

Cover Reveal: ____

ARC Release: ____

Send to Pre-Reader(s) By: ____

Send to Blogs By: ____

Send to Betas By: ____

Send to Editor By: ____

Send to Formatter By: ____

Set Up Pre-Order/Release By: ____

Final Cover Design Needed By: ____

Upload By: ____

Extra Notes:

____

____

____

____

Book Title: _______________________________

Release Date: _______________________________

Cover Reveal: _______________________________

ARC Release: _______________________________

Send to Pre-Reader(s) By: _______________________________

Send to Blogs By: _______________________________

Send to Betas By: _______________________________

Send to Editor By: _______________________________

Send to Formatter By: _______________________________

Set Up Pre-Order/Release By: _______________________________

Final Cover Design Needed By: _______________________________

Upload By: _______________________________

Extra Notes:

____

____

____

____

Book Title: ______________________________

Release Date: ______________________________

Cover Reveal: ______________________________

ARC Release: ______________________________

Send to Pre-Reader(s) By: ______________________________

Send to Blogs By: ______________________________

Send to Betas By: ______________________________

Send to Editor By: ______________________________

Send to Formatter By: ______________________________

Set Up Pre-Order/Release By: ______________________________

Final Cover Design Needed By: ______________________________

Upload By: ______________________________

Extra Notes:

____

____

____

____

Book Title: ______________________________

Release Date: ______________________________

Cover Reveal: ______________________________

ARC Release: ______________________________

Send to Pre-Reader(s) By: ______________________________

Send to Blogs By: ______________________________

Send to Betas By: ______________________________

Send to Editor By: ______________________________

Send to Formatter By: ______________________________

Set Up Pre-Order/Release By: ______________________________

Final Cover Design Needed By: ______________________________

Upload By: ______________________________

Extra Notes:

____

____

____

____

Book Title: ___________________________________

Release Date: ___________________________________

Cover Reveal: ___________________________________

ARC Release: ___________________________________

Send to Pre-Reader(s) By: ___________________________________

Send to Blogs By: ___________________________________

Send to Betas By: ___________________________________

Send to Editor By: ___________________________________

Send to Formatter By: ___________________________________

Set Up Pre-Order/Release By: ___________________________________

Final Cover Design Needed By: ___________________________________

Upload By: ___________________________________

Extra Notes:

____

____

____

____

Book Title: ______________________________

Release Date: ______________________________

Cover Reveal: ______________________________

ARC Release: ______________________________

Send to Pre-Reader(s) By: ______________________________

Send to Blogs By: ______________________________

Send to Betas By: ______________________________

Send to Editor By: ______________________________

Send to Formatter By: ______________________________

Set Up Pre-Order/Release By: ______________________________

Final Cover Design Needed By: ______________________________

Upload By: ______________________________

Extra Notes:

____

____

____

____

____

Book Title: ______________________________

Release Date: ______________________________

Cover Reveal: ______________________________

ARC Release: ______________________________

Send to Pre-Reader(s) By: ______________________________

Send to Blogs By: ______________________________

Send to Betas By: ______________________________

Send to Editor By: ______________________________

Send to Formatter By: ______________________________

Set Up Pre-Order/Release By: ______________________________

Final Cover Design Needed By: ______________________________

Upload By: ______________________________

Extra Notes:

____

____

____

____

____

Book Title: ______________________________________

Release Date: ______________________________________

Cover Reveal: ______________________________________

ARC Release: ______________________________________

Send to Pre-Reader(s) By: ______________________________________

Send to Blogs By: ______________________________________

Send to Betas By: ______________________________________

Send to Editor By: ______________________________________

Send to Formatter By: ______________________________________

Set Up Pre-Order/Release By: ______________________________________

Final Cover Design Needed By: ______________________________________

Upload By: ______________________________________

Extra Notes:

____

____

____

____

____

Book Title: _______________________________________

Release Date: _______________________________________

Cover Reveal: _______________________________________

ARC Release: _______________________________________

Send to Pre-Reader(s) By: _______________________________________

Send to Blogs By: _______________________________________

Send to Betas By: _______________________________________

Send to Editor By: _______________________________________

Send to Formatter By: _______________________________________

Set Up Pre-Order/Release By: _______________________________________

Final Cover Design Needed By: _______________________________________

Upload By: _______________________________________

Extra Notes:

____

____

____

____

Book Title: _______________________________

Release Date: _______________________________

Cover Reveal: _______________________________

ARC Release: _______________________________

Send to Pre-Reader(s) By: _______________________________

Send to Blogs By: _______________________________

Send to Betas By: _______________________________

Send to Editor By: _______________________________

Send to Formatter By: _______________________________

Set Up Pre-Order/Release By: _______________________________

Final Cover Design Needed By: _______________________________

Upload By: _______________________________

Extra Notes:

____

____

____

____

____

Book Title: ____

Release Date: ____

Cover Reveal: ____

ARC Release: ____

Send to Pre-Reader(s) By: ____

Send to Blogs By: ____

Send to Betas By: ____

Send to Editor By: ____

Send to Formatter By: ____

Set Up Pre-Order/Release By: ____

Final Cover Design Needed By: ____

Upload By: ____

Extra Notes:

____

____

____

____

____

Book Title: ___________________________________

Release Date: ___________________________________

Cover Reveal: ___________________________________

ARC Release: ___________________________________

Send to Pre-Reader(s) By: ___________________________________

Send to Blogs By: ___________________________________

Send to Betas By: ___________________________________

Send to Editor By: ___________________________________

Send to Formatter By: ___________________________________

Set Up Pre-Order/Release By: ___________________________________

Final Cover Design Needed By: ___________________________________

Upload By: ___________________________________

Extra Notes:

____

____

____

____

Book Title: ______________________________

Release Date: ______________________________

Cover Reveal: ______________________________

ARC Release: ______________________________

Send to Pre-Reader(s) By: ______________________________

Send to Blogs By: ______________________________

Send to Betas By: ______________________________

Send to Editor By: ______________________________

Send to Formatter By: ______________________________

Set Up Pre-Order/Release By: ______________________________

Final Cover Design Needed By: ______________________________

Upload By: ______________________________

Extra Notes:

____

____

____

____

Book Title: _______________________________________

Release Date: _______________________________________

Cover Reveal: _______________________________________

ARC Release: _______________________________________

Send to Pre-Reader(s) By: _______________________________________

Send to Blogs By: _______________________________________

Send to Betas By: _______________________________________

Send to Editor By: _______________________________________

Send to Formatter By: _______________________________________

Set Up Pre-Order/Release By: _______________________________________

Final Cover Design Needed By: _______________________________________

Upload By: _______________________________________

Extra Notes:

____

____

____

____

____

Book Title: _______________________________________

Release Date: _______________________________________

Cover Reveal: _______________________________________

ARC Release: _______________________________________

Send to Pre-Reader(s) By: _______________________________________

Send to Blogs By: _______________________________________

Send to Betas By: _______________________________________

Send to Editor By: _______________________________________

Send to Formatter By: _______________________________________

Set Up Pre-Order/Release By: _______________________________________

Final Cover Design Needed By: _______________________________________

Upload By: _______________________________________

Extra Notes:

____

____

____

____

____

Book Title: _______________________________________

Release Date: _______________________________________

Cover Reveal: _______________________________________

ARC Release: _______________________________________

Send to Pre-Reader(s) By: _______________________________________

Send to Blogs By: _______________________________________

Send to Betas By: _______________________________________

Send to Editor By: _______________________________________

Send to Formatter By: _______________________________________

Set Up Pre-Order/Release By: _______________________________________

Final Cover Design Needed By: _______________________________________

Upload By: _______________________________________

Extra Notes:

____

____

____

____

Book Title: ____

Release Date: ____

Cover Reveal: ____

ARC Release: ____

Send to Pre-Reader(s) By: ____

Send to Blogs By: ____

Send to Betas By: ____

Send to Editor By: ____

Send to Formatter By: ____

Set Up Pre-Order/Release By: ____

Final Cover Design Needed By: ____

Upload By: ____

Extra Notes:

____

____

____

____

Book Title: ______________________________________

Release Date: ______________________________________

Cover Reveal: ______________________________________

ARC Release: ______________________________________

Send to Pre-Reader(s) By: ______________________________________

Send to Blogs By: ______________________________________

Send to Betas By: ______________________________________

Send to Editor By: ______________________________________

Send to Formatter By: ______________________________________

Set Up Pre-Order/Release By: ______________________________________

Final Cover Design Needed By: ______________________________________

Upload By: ______________________________________

Extra Notes:

____

____

____

____

____

Book Title: ______________________________________

Release Date: ______________________________________

Cover Reveal: ______________________________________

ARC Release: ______________________________________

Send to Pre-Reader(s) By: ______________________________________

Send to Blogs By: ______________________________________

Send to Betas By: ______________________________________

Send to Editor By: ______________________________________

Send to Formatter By: ______________________________________

Set Up Pre-Order/Release By: ______________________________________

Final Cover Design Needed By: ______________________________________

Upload By: ______________________________________

Extra Notes:

____

____

____

____

Book Title: _______________________________

Release Date: _______________________________

Cover Reveal: _______________________________

ARC Release: _______________________________

Send to Pre-Reader(s) By: _______________________________

Send to Blogs By: _______________________________

Send to Betas By: _______________________________

Send to Editor By: _______________________________

Send to Formatter By: _______________________________

Set Up Pre-Order/Release By: _______________________________

Final Cover Design Needed By: _______________________________

Upload By: _______________________________

Extra Notes:

____

____

____

____

____

Book Title: ___________________________________

Release Date: ___________________________________

Cover Reveal: ___________________________________

ARC Release: ___________________________________

Send to Pre-Reader(s) By: ___________________________________

Send to Blogs By: ___________________________________

Send to Betas By: ___________________________________

Send to Editor By: ___________________________________

Send to Formatter By: ___________________________________

Set Up Pre-Order/Release By: ___________________________________

Final Cover Design Needed By: ___________________________________

Upload By: ___________________________________

Extra Notes:

____

____

____

____

____

Book Title: _______________________________________

Release Date: _______________________________________

Cover Reveal: _______________________________________

ARC Release: _______________________________________

Send to Pre-Reader(s) By: _________________________________

Send to Blogs By: _________________________________

Send to Betas By: _________________________________

Send to Editor By: _________________________________

Send to Formatter By: _________________________________

Set Up Pre-Order/Release By: _________________________________

Final Cover Design Needed By: ________________________________

Upload By: _________________________________

Extra Notes:

____

____

____

____

Book Title: ______________________________

Release Date: ______________________________

Cover Reveal: ______________________________

ARC Release: ______________________________

Send to Pre-Reader(s) By: ______________________________

Send to Blogs By: ______________________________

Send to Betas By: ______________________________

Send to Editor By: ______________________________

Send to Formatter By: ______________________________

Set Up Pre-Order/Release By: ______________________________

Final Cover Design Needed By: ______________________________

Upload By: ______________________________

Extra Notes:

____

____

____

____

____

Book Title: _______________________________

Release Date: _______________________________

Cover Reveal: _______________________________

ARC Release: _______________________________

Send to Pre-Reader(s) By: _______________________________

Send to Blogs By: _______________________________

Send to Betas By: _______________________________

Send to Editor By: _______________________________

Send to Formatter By: _______________________________

Set Up Pre-Order/Release By: _______________________________

Final Cover Design Needed By: _______________________________

Upload By: _______________________________

Extra Notes:

____

____

____

____

Book Title: ______________________________________

Release Date: ______________________________________

Cover Reveal: ______________________________________

ARC Release: ______________________________________

Send to Pre-Reader(s) By: ______________________________________

Send to Blogs By: ______________________________________

Send to Betas By: ______________________________________

Send to Editor By: ______________________________________

Send to Formatter By: ______________________________________

Set Up Pre-Order/Release By: ______________________________________

Final Cover Design Needed By: ______________________________________

Upload By: ______________________________________

Extra Notes:

____

____

____

____

Book Title: ____

Release Date: ____

Cover Reveal: ____

ARC Release: ____

Send to Pre-Reader(s) By: ____

Send to Blogs By: ____

Send to Betas By: ____

Send to Editor By: ____

Send to Formatter By: ____

Set Up Pre-Order/Release By: ____

Final Cover Design Needed By: ____

Upload By: ____

Extra Notes:

____

____

____

____

Book Title: ___________________________________

Release Date: ___________________________________

Cover Reveal: ___________________________________

ARC Release: ___________________________________

Send to Pre-Reader(s) By: ___________________________________

Send to Blogs By: ___________________________________

Send to Betas By: ___________________________________

Send to Editor By: ___________________________________

Send to Formatter By: ___________________________________

Set Up Pre-Order/Release By: ___________________________________

Final Cover Design Needed By: ___________________________________

Upload By: ___________________________________

Extra Notes:

____

____

____

____

____

Book Title: _______________________________

Release Date: _______________________________

Cover Reveal: _______________________________

ARC Release: _______________________________

Send to Pre-Reader(s) By: _______________________________

Send to Blogs By: _______________________________

Send to Betas By: _______________________________

Send to Editor By: _______________________________

Send to Formatter By: _______________________________

Set Up Pre-Order/Release By: _______________________________

Final Cover Design Needed By: _______________________________

Upload By: _______________________________

Extra Notes:

____

____

____

____

Book Title: ______________________________________

Release Date: ______________________________________

Cover Reveal: ______________________________________

ARC Release: ______________________________________

Send to Pre-Reader(s) By: ______________________________________

Send to Blogs By: ______________________________________

Send to Betas By: ______________________________________

Send to Editor By: ______________________________________

Send to Formatter By: ______________________________________

Set Up Pre-Order/Release By: ______________________________________

Final Cover Design Needed By: ______________________________________

Upload By: ______________________________________

Extra Notes:

____

____

____

____

Book Title: ______________________________

Release Date: ______________________________

Cover Reveal: ______________________________

ARC Release: ______________________________

Send to Pre-Reader(s) By: ______________________________

Send to Blogs By: ______________________________

Send to Betas By: ______________________________

Send to Editor By: ______________________________

Send to Formatter By: ______________________________

Set Up Pre-Order/Release By: ______________________________

Final Cover Design Needed By: ______________________________

Upload By: ______________________________

Extra Notes:

____

____

____

____

____

Book Title: _______________________________________

Release Date: _______________________________________

Cover Reveal: _______________________________________

ARC Release: _______________________________________

Send to Pre-Reader(s) By: _______________________________________

Send to Blogs By: _______________________________________

Send to Betas By: _______________________________________

Send to Editor By: _______________________________________

Send to Formatter By: _______________________________________

Set Up Pre-Order/Release By: _______________________________________

Final Cover Design Needed By: _______________________________________

Upload By: _______________________________________

Extra Notes:

____

____

____

____

____

Book Title: _______________________________

Release Date: _______________________________

Cover Reveal: _______________________________

ARC Release: _______________________________

Send to Pre-Reader(s) By: _______________________________

Send to Blogs By: _______________________________

Send to Betas By: _______________________________

Send to Editor By: _______________________________

Send to Formatter By: _______________________________

Set Up Pre-Order/Release By: _______________________________

Final Cover Design Needed By: _______________________________

Upload By: _______________________________

Extra Notes:

____

____

____

____

Book Title: ______________________________

Release Date: ______________________________

Cover Reveal: ______________________________

ARC Release: ______________________________

Send to Pre-Reader(s) By: ______________________________

Send to Blogs By: ______________________________

Send to Betas By: ______________________________

Send to Editor By: ______________________________

Send to Formatter By: ______________________________

Set Up Pre-Order/Release By: ______________________________

Final Cover Design Needed By: ______________________________

Upload By: ______________________________

Extra Notes:

____

____

____

____

Book Title: ______________________________

Release Date: ______________________________

Cover Reveal: ______________________________

ARC Release: ______________________________

Send to Pre-Reader(s) By: ______________________________

Send to Blogs By: ______________________________

Send to Betas By: ______________________________

Send to Editor By: ______________________________

Send to Formatter By: ______________________________

Set Up Pre-Order/Release By: ______________________________

Final Cover Design Needed By: ______________________________

Upload By: ______________________________

Extra Notes:

____

____

____

____

____

Book Title: ________________________________

Release Date: ________________________________

Cover Reveal: ________________________________

ARC Release: ________________________________

Send to Pre-Reader(s) By: __________________________

Send to Blogs By: ________________________________

Send to Betas By: ________________________________

Send to Editor By: ______________________________

Send to Formatter By: ___________________________

Set Up Pre-Order/Release By: _________________________

Final Cover Design Needed By: ________________________

Upload By: ________________________________

Extra Notes:

____

____

____

____

____

Book Title: _______________________________

Release Date: _______________________________

Cover Reveal: _______________________________

ARC Release: _______________________________

Send to Pre-Reader(s) By: _______________________________

Send to Blogs By: _______________________________

Send to Betas By: _______________________________

Send to Editor By: _______________________________

Send to Formatter By: _______________________________

Set Up Pre-Order/Release By: _______________________________

Final Cover Design Needed By: _______________________________

Upload By: _______________________________

Extra Notes:

____

____

____

____

____

Book Title: _______________________________

Release Date: _______________________________

Cover Reveal: _______________________________

ARC Release: _______________________________

Send to Pre-Reader(s) By: _______________________________

Send to Blogs By: _______________________________

Send to Betas By: _______________________________

Send to Editor By: _______________________________

Send to Formatter By: _______________________________

Set Up Pre-Order/Release By: _______________________________

Final Cover Design Needed By: _______________________________

Upload By: _______________________________

Extra Notes:

____

____

____

____

Book Title: ______________________________

Release Date: ______________________________

Cover Reveal: ______________________________

ARC Release: ______________________________

Send to Pre-Reader(s) By: ______________________________

Send to Blogs By: ______________________________

Send to Betas By: ______________________________

Send to Editor By: ______________________________

Send to Formatter By: ______________________________

Set Up Pre-Order/Release By: ______________________________

Final Cover Design Needed By: ______________________________

Upload By: ______________________________

Extra Notes:

____

____

____

____

Book Title: _______________________________

Release Date: _______________________________

Cover Reveal: _______________________________

ARC Release: _______________________________

Send to Pre-Reader(s) By: _______________________________

Send to Blogs By: _______________________________

Send to Betas By: _______________________________

Send to Editor By: _______________________________

Send to Formatter By: _______________________________

Set Up Pre-Order/Release By: _______________________________

Final Cover Design Needed By: _______________________________

Upload By: _______________________________

Extra Notes:

____

____

____

____

____

Book Title: _______________________________________

Release Date: _______________________________________

Cover Reveal: _______________________________________

ARC Release: _______________________________________

Send to Pre-Reader(s) By: _______________________________________

Send to Blogs By: _______________________________________

Send to Betas By: _______________________________________

Send to Editor By: _______________________________________

Send to Formatter By: _______________________________________

Set Up Pre-Order/Release By: _______________________________________

Final Cover Design Needed By: _______________________________________

Upload By: _______________________________________

Extra Notes:

____

____

____

____

Book Title: ______________________________

Release Date: ______________________________

Cover Reveal: ______________________________

ARC Release: ______________________________

Send to Pre-Reader(s) By: ______________________________

Send to Blogs By: ______________________________

Send to Betas By: ______________________________

Send to Editor By: ______________________________

Send to Formatter By: ______________________________

Set Up Pre-Order/Release By: ______________________________

Final Cover Design Needed By: ______________________________

Upload By: ______________________________

Extra Notes:

____

____

____

____

____

Book Title: _______________________________

Release Date: _______________________________

Cover Reveal: _______________________________

ARC Release: _______________________________

Send to Pre-Reader(s) By: _______________________________

Send to Blogs By: _______________________________

Send to Betas By: _______________________________

Send to Editor By: _______________________________

Send to Formatter By: _______________________________

Set Up Pre-Order/Release By: _______________________________

Final Cover Design Needed By: _______________________________

Upload By: _______________________________

Extra Notes:

____

____

____

____

Book Title: ___________________________________

Release Date: ___________________________________

Cover Reveal: ___________________________________

ARC Release: ___________________________________

Send to Pre-Reader(s) By: ___________________________________

Send to Blogs By: ___________________________________

Send to Betas By: ___________________________________

Send to Editor By: ___________________________________

Send to Formatter By: ___________________________________

Set Up Pre-Order/Release By: ___________________________________

Final Cover Design Needed By: ___________________________________

Upload By: ___________________________________

Extra Notes:

____

____

____

____

____

Book Title: _______________________________

Release Date: _______________________________

Cover Reveal: _______________________________

ARC Release: _______________________________

Send to Pre-Reader(s) By: _______________________________

Send to Blogs By: _______________________________

Send to Betas By: _______________________________

Send to Editor By: _______________________________

Send to Formatter By: _______________________________

Set Up Pre-Order/Release By: _______________________________

Final Cover Design Needed By: _______________________________

Upload By: _______________________________

Extra Notes:

____

____

____

____

Book Title: ____

Release Date: ____

Cover Reveal: ____

ARC Release: ____

Send to Pre-Reader(s) By: ____

Send to Blogs By: ____

Send to Betas By: ____

Send to Editor By: ____

Send to Formatter By: ____

Set Up Pre-Order/Release By: ____

Final Cover Design Needed By: ____

Upload By: ____

Extra Notes:

____

____

____

____

Book Title: _______________________________

Release Date: _______________________________

Cover Reveal: _______________________________

ARC Release: _______________________________

Send to Pre-Reader(s) By: _______________________________

Send to Blogs By: _______________________________

Send to Betas By: _______________________________

Send to Editor By: _______________________________

Send to Formatter By: _______________________________

Set Up Pre-Order/Release By: _______________________________

Final Cover Design Needed By: _______________________________

Upload By: _______________________________

Extra Notes:

____

____

____

____

Book Title: ______________________________

Release Date: ______________________________

Cover Reveal: ______________________________

ARC Release: ______________________________

Send to Pre-Reader(s) By: ______________________________

Send to Blogs By: ______________________________

Send to Betas By: ______________________________

Send to Editor By: ______________________________

Send to Formatter By: ______________________________

Set Up Pre-Order/Release By: ______________________________

Final Cover Design Needed By: ______________________________

Upload By: ______________________________

Extra Notes:

____

____

____

____

____

Book Title: ___________________________

Release Date: ___________________________

Cover Reveal: ___________________________

ARC Release: ___________________________

Send to Pre-Reader(s) By: ___________________________

Send to Blogs By: ___________________________

Send to Betas By: ___________________________

Send to Editor By: ___________________________

Send to Formatter By: ___________________________

Set Up Pre-Order/Release By: ___________________________

Final Cover Design Needed By: ___________________________

Upload By: ___________________________

Extra Notes:

____

____

____

____

Book Title: _______________________________

Release Date: _______________________________

Cover Reveal: _______________________________

ARC Release: _______________________________

Send to Pre-Reader(s) By: _______________________________

Send to Blogs By: _______________________________

Send to Betas By: _______________________________

Send to Editor By: _______________________________

Send to Formatter By: _______________________________

Set Up Pre-Order/Release By: _______________________________

Final Cover Design Needed By: _______________________________

Upload By: _______________________________

Extra Notes:

____

____

____

____

____

Book Title: _______________________________

Release Date: _______________________________

Cover Reveal: _______________________________

ARC Release: _______________________________

Send to Pre-Reader(s) By: _______________________________

Send to Blogs By: _______________________________

Send to Betas By: _______________________________

Send to Editor By: _______________________________

Send to Formatter By: _______________________________

Set Up Pre-Order/Release By: _______________________________

Final Cover Design Needed By: _______________________________

Upload By: _______________________________

Extra Notes:

____

____

____

____

Book Title: ______________________________

Release Date: ______________________________

Cover Reveal: ______________________________

ARC Release: ______________________________

Send to Pre-Reader(s) By: ______________________________

Send to Blogs By: ______________________________

Send to Betas By: ______________________________

Send to Editor By: ______________________________

Send to Formatter By: ______________________________

Set Up Pre-Order/Release By: ______________________________

Final Cover Design Needed By: ______________________________

Upload By: ______________________________

Extra Notes:

____

____

____

____

Book Title: ____

Release Date: ____

Cover Reveal: ____

ARC Release: ____

Send to Pre-Reader(s) By: ____

Send to Blogs By: ____

Send to Betas By: ____

Send to Editor By: ____

Send to Formatter By: ____

Set Up Pre-Order/Release By: ____

Final Cover Design Needed By: ____

Upload By: ____

Extra Notes:

____

____

____

____

Book Title: _______________________________

Release Date: _______________________________

Cover Reveal: _______________________________

ARC Release: _______________________________

Send to Pre-Reader(s) By: _______________________________

Send to Blogs By: _______________________________

Send to Betas By: _______________________________

Send to Editor By: _______________________________

Send to Formatter By: _______________________________

Set Up Pre-Order/Release By: _______________________________

Final Cover Design Needed By: _______________________________

Upload By: _______________________________

Extra Notes:

____

____

____

____

Book Title: _______________________________

Release Date: _______________________________

Cover Reveal: _______________________________

ARC Release: _______________________________

Send to Pre-Reader(s) By: _______________________________

Send to Blogs By: _______________________________

Send to Betas By: _______________________________

Send to Editor By: _______________________________

Send to Formatter By: _______________________________

Set Up Pre-Order/Release By: _______________________________

Final Cover Design Needed By: _______________________________

Upload By: _______________________________

Extra Notes:

____

____

____

____

Book Title: ________________________________

Release Date: ________________________________

Cover Reveal: ________________________________

ARC Release: ________________________________

Send to Pre-Reader(s) By: ________________________________

Send to Blogs By: ________________________________

Send to Betas By: ________________________________

Send to Editor By: ________________________________

Send to Formatter By: ________________________________

Set Up Pre-Order/Release By: ________________________________

Final Cover Design Needed By: ________________________________

Upload By: ________________________________

Extra Notes:

____

____

____

____

____

Book Title: _______________________________

Release Date: _______________________________

Cover Reveal: _______________________________

ARC Release: _______________________________

Send to Pre-Reader(s) By: _______________________________

Send to Blogs By: _______________________________

Send to Betas By: _______________________________

Send to Editor By: _______________________________

Send to Formatter By: _______________________________

Set Up Pre-Order/Release By: _______________________________

Final Cover Design Needed By: _______________________________

Upload By: _______________________________

Extra Notes:

____

____

____

____

____

Book Title: ______________________________

Release Date: ______________________________

Cover Reveal: ______________________________

ARC Release: ______________________________

Send to Pre-Reader(s) By: ______________________________

Send to Blogs By: ______________________________

Send to Betas By: ______________________________

Send to Editor By: ______________________________

Send to Formatter By: ______________________________

Set Up Pre-Order/Release By: ______________________________

Final Cover Design Needed By: ______________________________

Upload By: ______________________________

Extra Notes:

____

____

____

____

Book Title: ______________________________

Release Date: ______________________________

Cover Reveal: ______________________________

ARC Release: ______________________________

Send to Pre-Reader(s) By: ______________________________

Send to Blogs By: ______________________________

Send to Betas By: ______________________________

Send to Editor By: ______________________________

Send to Formatter By: ______________________________

Set Up Pre-Order/Release By: ______________________________

Final Cover Design Needed By: ______________________________

Upload By: ______________________________

Extra Notes:

____

____

____

____

____

Book Title: ___________________________

Release Date: ___________________________

Cover Reveal: ___________________________

ARC Release: ___________________________

Send to Pre-Reader(s) By: ___________________________

Send to Blogs By: ___________________________

Send to Betas By: ___________________________

Send to Editor By: ___________________________

Send to Formatter By: ___________________________

Set Up Pre-Order/Release By: ___________________________

Final Cover Design Needed By: ___________________________

Upload By: ___________________________

Extra Notes:

____

____

____

____

Book Title: _______________________________________

Release Date: _______________________________________

Cover Reveal: _______________________________________

ARC Release: _______________________________________

Send to Pre-Reader(s) By: _______________________________________

Send to Blogs By: _______________________________________

Send to Betas By: _______________________________________

Send to Editor By: _______________________________________

Send to Formatter By: _______________________________________

Set Up Pre-Order/Release By: _______________________________________

Final Cover Design Needed By: _______________________________________

Upload By: _______________________________________

Extra Notes:

____

____

____

____

____

Book Title: ______________________________________

Release Date: ______________________________________

Cover Reveal: ______________________________________

ARC Release: ______________________________________

Send to Pre-Reader(s) By: ______________________________________

Send to Blogs By: ______________________________________

Send to Betas By: ______________________________________

Send to Editor By: ______________________________________

Send to Formatter By: ______________________________________

Set Up Pre-Order/Release By: ______________________________________

Final Cover Design Needed By: ______________________________________

Upload By: ______________________________________

Extra Notes:

____

____

____

____

Book Title: _______________________________

Release Date: _______________________________

Cover Reveal: _______________________________

ARC Release: _______________________________

Send to Pre-Reader(s) By: _______________________________

Send to Blogs By: _______________________________

Send to Betas By: _______________________________

Send to Editor By: _______________________________

Send to Formatter By: _______________________________

Set Up Pre-Order/Release By: _______________________________

Final Cover Design Needed By: _______________________________

Upload By: _______________________________

Extra Notes:

____

____

____

____

____

Book Title: _____________________________________

Release Date: _____________________________________

Cover Reveal: _____________________________________

ARC Release: _____________________________________

Send to Pre-Reader(s) By: _____________________________________

Send to Blogs By: _____________________________________

Send to Betas By: _____________________________________

Send to Editor By: _____________________________________

Send to Formatter By: _____________________________________

Set Up Pre-Order/Release By: _____________________________________

Final Cover Design Needed By: _____________________________________

Upload By: _____________________________________

Extra Notes:

____

____

____

____

____

Book Title: ______________________________

Release Date: ______________________________

Cover Reveal: ______________________________

ARC Release: ______________________________

Send to Pre-Reader(s) By: ______________________________

Send to Blogs By: ______________________________

Send to Betas By: ______________________________

Send to Editor By: ______________________________

Send to Formatter By: ______________________________

Set Up Pre-Order/Release By: ______________________________

Final Cover Design Needed By: ______________________________

Upload By: ______________________________

Extra Notes:

____

____

____

____

Book Title: ______________________________

Release Date: ______________________________

Cover Reveal: ______________________________

ARC Release: ______________________________

Send to Pre-Reader(s) By: ______________________________

Send to Blogs By: ______________________________

Send to Betas By: ______________________________

Send to Editor By: ______________________________

Send to Formatter By: ______________________________

Set Up Pre-Order/Release By: ______________________________

Final Cover Design Needed By: ______________________________

Upload By: ______________________________

Extra Notes:

____

____

____

____

____

Book Title: _______________________________________

Release Date: _______________________________________

Cover Reveal: _______________________________________

ARC Release: _______________________________________

Send to Pre-Reader(s) By: _______________________________________

Send to Blogs By: _______________________________________

Send to Betas By: _______________________________________

Send to Editor By: _______________________________________

Send to Formatter By: _______________________________________

Set Up Pre-Order/Release By: _______________________________________

Final Cover Design Needed By: _______________________________________

Upload By: _______________________________________

Extra Notes:

____

____

____

____

Book Title: _______________________________________

Release Date: _______________________________________

Cover Reveal: _______________________________________

ARC Release: _______________________________________

Send to Pre-Reader(s) By: _______________________________________

Send to Blogs By: _______________________________________

Send to Betas By: _______________________________________

Send to Editor By: _______________________________________

Send to Formatter By: _______________________________________

Set Up Pre-Order/Release By: _______________________________________

Final Cover Design Needed By: _______________________________________

Upload By: _______________________________________

Extra Notes:

____

____

____

____

Book Title: _______________________________________

Release Date: _______________________________________

Cover Reveal: _______________________________________

ARC Release: _______________________________________

Send to Pre-Reader(s) By: _______________________________________

Send to Blogs By: _______________________________________

Send to Betas By: _______________________________________

Send to Editor By: _______________________________________

Send to Formatter By: _______________________________________

Set Up Pre-Order/Release By: _______________________________________

Final Cover Design Needed By: _______________________________________

Upload By: _______________________________________

Extra Notes:

____

____

____

____

____

Book Title: ___________________________________

Release Date: ___________________________________

Cover Reveal: ___________________________________

ARC Release: ___________________________________

Send to Pre-Reader(s) By: ___________________________________

Send to Blogs By: ___________________________________

Send to Betas By: ___________________________________

Send to Editor By: ___________________________________

Send to Formatter By: ___________________________________

Set Up Pre-Order/Release By: ___________________________________

Final Cover Design Needed By: ___________________________________

Upload By: ___________________________________

Extra Notes:

____

____

____

____

Book Title: _______________________________

Release Date: _______________________________

Cover Reveal: _______________________________

ARC Release: _______________________________

Send to Pre-Reader(s) By: _______________________________

Send to Blogs By: _______________________________

Send to Betas By: _______________________________

Send to Editor By: _______________________________

Send to Formatter By: _______________________________

Set Up Pre-Order/Release By: _______________________________

Final Cover Design Needed By: _______________________________

Upload By: _______________________________

Extra Notes:

____

____

____

____

Book Title: _______________________________________

Release Date: _______________________________________

Cover Reveal: _______________________________________

ARC Release: _______________________________________

Send to Pre-Reader(s) By: _______________________________________

Send to Blogs By: _______________________________________

Send to Betas By: _______________________________________

Send to Editor By: _______________________________________

Send to Formatter By: _______________________________________

Set Up Pre-Order/Release By: _______________________________________

Final Cover Design Needed By: _______________________________________

Upload By: _______________________________________

Extra Notes:

____

____

____

____

____

Book Title: ______________________________

Release Date: ______________________________

Cover Reveal: ______________________________

ARC Release: ______________________________

Send to Pre-Reader(s) By: ______________________________

Send to Blogs By: ______________________________

Send to Betas By: ______________________________

Send to Editor By: ______________________________

Send to Formatter By: ______________________________

Set Up Pre-Order/Release By: ______________________________

Final Cover Design Needed By: ______________________________

Upload By: ______________________________

Extra Notes:

____

____

____

____

Book Title: ___________________________________

Release Date: ___________________________________

Cover Reveal: ___________________________________

ARC Release: ___________________________________

Send to Pre-Reader(s) By: ___________________________________

Send to Blogs By: ___________________________________

Send to Betas By: ___________________________________

Send to Editor By: ___________________________________

Send to Formatter By: ___________________________________

Set Up Pre-Order/Release By: ___________________________________

Final Cover Design Needed By: ___________________________________

Upload By: ___________________________________

Extra Notes:

____

____

____

____

____

Book Title: _______________________________

Release Date: _______________________________

Cover Reveal: _______________________________

ARC Release: _______________________________

Send to Pre-Reader(s) By: _______________________________

Send to Blogs By: _______________________________

Send to Betas By: _______________________________

Send to Editor By: _______________________________

Send to Formatter By: _______________________________

Set Up Pre-Order/Release By: _______________________________

Final Cover Design Needed By: _______________________________

Upload By: _______________________________

Extra Notes:

____

____

____

____

Book Title: __________________________

Release Date: __________________________

Cover Reveal: __________________________

ARC Release: __________________________

Send to Pre-Reader(s) By: __________________________

Send to Blogs By: __________________________

Send to Betas By: __________________________

Send to Editor By: __________________________

Send to Formatter By: __________________________

Set Up Pre-Order/Release By: __________________________

Final Cover Design Needed By: __________________________

Upload By: __________________________

Extra Notes:

____

____

____

____

____

Book Title: ______________________________

Release Date: ______________________________

Cover Reveal: ______________________________

ARC Release: ______________________________

Send to Pre-Reader(s) By: ______________________________

Send to Blogs By: ______________________________

Send to Betas By: ______________________________

Send to Editor By: ______________________________

Send to Formatter By: ______________________________

Set Up Pre-Order/Release By: ______________________________

Final Cover Design Needed By: ______________________________

Upload By: ______________________________

Extra Notes:

____

____

____

____

Book Title: ___________________________________

Release Date: ___________________________________

Cover Reveal: ___________________________________

ARC Release: ___________________________________

Send to Pre-Reader(s) By: ___________________________________

Send to Blogs By: ___________________________________

Send to Betas By: ___________________________________

Send to Editor By: ___________________________________

Send to Formatter By: ___________________________________

Set Up Pre-Order/Release By: ___________________________________

Final Cover Design Needed By: ___________________________________

Upload By: ___________________________________

Extra Notes:

____

____

____

____

____

Book Title: ______________________________

Release Date: ______________________________

Cover Reveal: ______________________________

ARC Release: ______________________________

Send to Pre-Reader(s) By: ______________________________

Send to Blogs By: ______________________________

Send to Betas By: ______________________________

Send to Editor By: ______________________________

Send to Formatter By: ______________________________

Set Up Pre-Order/Release By: ______________________________

Final Cover Design Needed By: ______________________________

Upload By: ______________________________

Extra Notes:

____

____

____

____

____

Book Title: ______________________________

Release Date: ______________________________

Cover Reveal: ______________________________

ARC Release: ______________________________

Send to Pre-Reader(s) By: ______________________________

Send to Blogs By: ______________________________

Send to Betas By: ______________________________

Send to Editor By: ______________________________

Send to Formatter By: ______________________________

Set Up Pre-Order/Release By: ______________________________

Final Cover Design Needed By: ______________________________

Upload By: ______________________________

Extra Notes:

____

____

____

____

Book Title: ___________________________________

Release Date: ___________________________________

Cover Reveal: ___________________________________

ARC Release: ___________________________________

Send to Pre-Reader(s) By: ___________________________________

Send to Blogs By: ___________________________________

Send to Betas By: ___________________________________

Send to Editor By: ___________________________________

Send to Formatter By: ___________________________________

Set Up Pre-Order/Release By: ___________________________________

Final Cover Design Needed By: ___________________________________

Upload By: ___________________________________

Extra Notes:

____

____

____

____

____

Book Title: ___________________________________

Release Date: ___________________________________

Cover Reveal: ___________________________________

ARC Release: ___________________________________

Send to Pre-Reader(s) By: ___________________________________

Send to Blogs By: ___________________________________

Send to Betas By: ___________________________________

Send to Editor By: ___________________________________

Send to Formatter By: ___________________________________

Set Up Pre-Order/Release By: ___________________________________

Final Cover Design Needed By: ___________________________________

Upload By: ___________________________________

Extra Notes:

____

____

____

____

Book Title: _______________________________________

Release Date: _______________________________________

Cover Reveal: _______________________________________

ARC Release: _______________________________________

Send to Pre-Reader(s) By: _______________________________________

Send to Blogs By: _______________________________________

Send to Betas By: _______________________________________

Send to Editor By: _______________________________________

Send to Formatter By: _______________________________________

Set Up Pre-Order/Release By: _______________________________________

Final Cover Design Needed By: _______________________________________

Upload By: _______________________________________

Extra Notes:

____

____

____

____

____

Book Title: _______________________________________

Release Date: _______________________________________

Cover Reveal: _______________________________________

ARC Release: _______________________________________

Send to Pre-Reader(s) By: _______________________________________

Send to Blogs By: _______________________________________

Send to Betas By: _______________________________________

Send to Editor By: _______________________________________

Send to Formatter By: _______________________________________

Set Up Pre-Order/Release By: _______________________________________

Final Cover Design Needed By: _______________________________________

Upload By: _______________________________________

Extra Notes:

____

____

____

____

____

Book Title: ______________________________

Release Date: ______________________________

Cover Reveal: ______________________________

ARC Release: ______________________________

Send to Pre-Reader(s) By: ______________________________

Send to Blogs By: ______________________________

Send to Betas By: ______________________________

Send to Editor By: ______________________________

Send to Formatter By: ______________________________

Set Up Pre-Order/Release By: ______________________________

Final Cover Design Needed By: ______________________________

Upload By: ______________________________

Extra Notes:

____

____

____

____

____

Book Title: _______________________________

Release Date: _______________________________

Cover Reveal: _______________________________

ARC Release: _______________________________

Send to Pre-Reader(s) By: _______________________________

Send to Blogs By: _______________________________

Send to Betas By: _______________________________

Send to Editor By: _______________________________

Send to Formatter By: _______________________________

Set Up Pre-Order/Release By: _______________________________

Final Cover Design Needed By: _______________________________

Upload By: _______________________________

Extra Notes:

____

____

____

____

Book Title: _______________________________

Release Date: _______________________________

Cover Reveal: _______________________________

ARC Release: _______________________________

Send to Pre-Reader(s) By: _______________________________

Send to Blogs By: _______________________________

Send to Betas By: _______________________________

Send to Editor By: _______________________________

Send to Formatter By: _______________________________

Set Up Pre-Order/Release By: _______________________________

Final Cover Design Needed By: _______________________________

Upload By: _______________________________

Extra Notes:

____

____

____

____

____

Book Title: _______________________________________

Release Date: _______________________________________

Cover Reveal: _______________________________________

ARC Release: _______________________________________

Send to Pre-Reader(s) By: _______________________________________

Send to Blogs By: _______________________________________

Send to Betas By: _______________________________________

Send to Editor By: _______________________________________

Send to Formatter By: _______________________________________

Set Up Pre-Order/Release By: _______________________________________

Final Cover Design Needed By: _______________________________________

Upload By: _______________________________________

Extra Notes:

____

____

____

____

____

Book Title: _______________________________

Release Date: _______________________________

Cover Reveal: _______________________________

ARC Release: _______________________________

Send to Pre-Reader(s) By: _______________________________

Send to Blogs By: _______________________________

Send to Betas By: _______________________________

Send to Editor By: _______________________________

Send to Formatter By: _______________________________

Set Up Pre-Order/Release By: _______________________________

Final Cover Design Needed By: _______________________________

Upload By: _______________________________

Extra Notes:

____

____

____

____

Book Title: ______________________________________

Release Date: ______________________________________

Cover Reveal: ______________________________________

ARC Release: ______________________________________

Send to Pre-Reader(s) By: ______________________________________

Send to Blogs By: ______________________________________

Send to Betas By: ______________________________________

Send to Editor By: ______________________________________

Send to Formatter By: ______________________________________

Set Up Pre-Order/Release By: ______________________________________

Final Cover Design Needed By: ______________________________________

Upload By: ______________________________________

Extra Notes:

____

____

____

____

Thank you so much for your purchase.

I really do hope that this book has helped you,
even in some small way.

Would you like to see different designs/styles?

I am always very happy to hear from customers,
so please feel free to email me on

teeceedesignstudio@yahoo.com